Brave Questions

Building Stronger Relationships
by Asking All the Right Questions

Dr. Alan R. Zimmerman

Brave Questions

Building Stronger Relationships
by Asking All the Right Questions

Dr. Alan R. Zimmerman

Published by:
Zimmerman Communi-Care Network, Inc.
20550 Lake Ridge Drive
Prior Lake, MN 55372

Cover design and layout: Ad Graphics, Inc., Tulsa, Oklahoma
Printed in the United States of America.

ISBN: 0-9656833-2-X

Table of Contents

* * * * *

Chapter One

The Discovery of Brave Questions

*T*his book will change your life. Its contents changed my life, and it will change yours.

MY WAKE-UP CALL

But let me explain. It was August, 1979, and I got a phone call from my father that changed my life forever. He was crying so hard that I could barely understand him. He had come home from work and found his wife's body. She had committed suicide.

That was just about the last thing I expected in life. Those things only happened to "other" people. Besides that, my mother was a great mother to me and a great wife to my father. She attended church, went to her bowling team, and everyone liked her. But she killed herself.

Two days after I lost my mother, I lost my wife. I found out she was getting a divorce. Of course, I had my share of the blame for the relationship falling apart, but it was one more thing I never expected to happen.

Talk about stress, change, and challenge. It was the big time. In the course of one weekend my world had fallen apart.

Nonetheless, my father and I proceeded with the funeral preparations. Everything about the funeral was "nice," and everyone who attended was "nice." My colleagues at the university sent some flowers. And that was "nice."

But something strange happened. When I went back to my professorship a few days later, nobody asked me anything. They were great colleagues, but they were taken off guard. They didn't know what to ask or even what to say. So they pretended nothing had happened in my life.

Of course we would talk, but it was always superficial. We'd talk about the weather, and they'd say, "Have a great day" and "See you around." But no one bothered—or no one dared—to ask any deeper questions about the monumental changes that had taken place in my life.

After six months of that, a professor from another department stopped me while I was walking across the campus one day. He said, "Just a minute, Alan. I know you've gone through a lot of changes in your life the last few months. I hope you don't mind if I ask, but I do care. I was just wondering how you're really doing."

I thought to myself, "Mind? Not at all." It felt great to have someone ask, "How are you doing?" and really mean the question. It felt so much better than all the other folks who asked "How are you?" and kept on walking before I answered.

My Observation

From that experience, I realized that many times we don't know what to ask our coworkers to build stronger work relationships. We don't even know what to ask our friends and family members much of the time.

So I began to watch people. I watched the professors and students at the university. I watched the people in organizations where I delivered seminars. And I watched the people in restaurants as I traveled across the country. I watched everyone.

I made the same observation everywhere. Lots of people don't know how to connect on a deeper level. Much of their communication is about the things they have to do and the people they know. The rest of their communication is focused on relatively unimportant topics such as the weather, the football game, and what's for dinner.

I noticed something especially interesting in restaurants. If I saw a man and woman leaning towards each other, talking and talking, I found out that more often than not, they weren't married.

By contrast, I noticed other restaurant couples who were looking around and hardly talking at all. And when they did talk, it was something superficial like, "How's your steak, Emily?" Strangely enough, these non-communicative couples were often the "married" couples.

I wondered what had happened. Why did so many couples start out with great communication, or at least pretty good communication, and end up with none?

After all, when those same "married" couples were dating, they probably had a million things to talk about. They were asking each other questions about the future, their hopes and dreams, and their thoughts on children, education, hobbies, careers, and everything else. In fact, saying "Good night" to one another at the end of a date felt like torture. They didn't want to stop talking or be apart. Then five or twenty five years later, those same two people may have difficulty talking on levels deeper than "How's your steak, Emily?"

So I wondered some more. I wondered what could be done to help people get through the challenges of life. I wondered what would keep their communication vital and alive. And I wondered what kind of communication would help team members and coworkers build greater trust and understanding.

THE ANSWER

The answer came a short time later. I was attending a five-day, personal-professional development program being led by Dr. Sidney Simon, a professor from the University of Massachusetts. It was by far one of the best workshops I had ever attended, and he was by far the best teacher I had ever encountered. I was impressed, to say the least.

Somewhere in the midst of the five days, Dr. Simon talked about "brave questions." "Brave questions" were deeper, gutsier, more personal questions than the ones we normally ask. And he said it worked best to do a series of twenty questions at a time. There was something about twenty that worked especially well in building open, honest communication.

Dr. Simon demonstrated. He asked for four volunteers from the workshop audience, two people who knew each other very well and two who had never met. They were instructed in the "brave question-20 questions" approach and encouraged to go for it, to take a risk, and give it a real try as the rest of us listened in.

It was awesome. In a matter of minutes, the couple who didn't know each other knew more about one another than friends they had "known" for years. And the couple who knew each other quite well experienced more closeness and understanding than they had in a long long time. All four of them were profoundly touched, and so were the rest of us in the audience.

A PERSONAL TRY

My first serious use of the "brave question-20 question" technique came in November, 1983. I was invited to a wedding along with my 83-year old grandmother. It was during our two-hour drive that I decided to "go for it."

I said, "Grandma, I've got a game I'd like to play. It's called '20 questions.' You can ask me anything at all, and I can ask you anything. Would that be okay? It will pass the time as we drive." She said, "Sure."

Now you have to realize that all my life I had known Grandma, but our conversations had always been superficial. We'd talk about the crafts she was making or what she was doing at the senior citizens' center, but we never talked about what she thought, how she felt, or what really counted in life.

As a result, I thought I'd start the process with a relatively easy question. I said, "Grandma, you've lived a long time. What was the happiest moment of your life?"

I didn't know what she would say. She replied, "I don't know the happiest moment. I've had many. But I can think of the most blessed moment. Would that be all right?" I said, "Of course."

She answered, "I don't know if you know this, but when I was 16 years of age, I was single and got pregnant." It stunned me. While it's not acceptable to be 16, single, and pregnant today, I could only imagine how awful that must have been some 70 years before in a small, conservative, Midwest farm town.

She continued, "My parents disowned me. I had nowhere to go. But a nearby farmer said I could stay in a room attached to his barn. The night I was giving birth, a midwife came over to help me. I was crying, feeling full of shame and remorse, saying my whole life was ruined."

But the midwife said, "I don't see it that way. You could have left town, tried to abort or cover your tracks so no one could have made fun of you. But you did what you thought was right. And for that I respect you."

Again I was stunned. I thought my first question for Grandma was an "easy" one that would bring a light answer. I was wrong. Our conversation went on and on as we continued our drive to the wedding.

And my understanding of the "brave question-20 question" process continued. I learned that when I ask brave questions and just listen to my partner's answers, the other person feels honored and special. I learned that the other person wants to keep on building the relationship. That became evident when my grandmother opened the next round of discussion.

A few months after our journey in the car, I was helping my grandmother with an auction. She was selling some of her household goods and moving to a smaller apartment. At the end of the day we talked about the items she sold and the prices she received. Then she said, "Alan, do you remember asking me all those questions in the car last year?" I said, "Yes." "Well," she said, "I didn't tell you everything. May I tell you more?" I replied, "Of course."

Grandma said, "When I got pregnant, I wasn't doing anything wrong. I had never had a date in my entire life. I stayed home and helped Ma and Pa with the chores on the farm. I milked the cows and churned the butter. But when I turned 16, there was a community dance. Pa said I could go."

She continued, "It was my first dance. I was so excited. One man asked me to dance, and then another and another. It was wonderful. One man asked if I'd like a ride home. I told him that would be nice."

As she shared the rest of her story, she talked about being raped on the way home. She tried to push the man away, to get him off her, but she couldn't do it. She said she had no recourse, because in those days, "You just didn't say anything." If such things happened, women were to blame. So no one would have believed her anyway.

I was surprised and saddened. She had been carrying her secret burden for 70 years. But our brave questions were building a trust and safety that allowed her to open up.

Before I asked "brave questions" and played "20 questions" with Grandma, we had a somewhat strained relationship.

She had a difficult, mean streak about her. She had even been abusive. I didn't know where her negative traits came from. I didn't know her background. I just knew she wasn't always the easiest person to be around.

Then something else started to happen. Through the questions I would ask, through the listening I would give her, Grandma began to change. She softened up and warmed up. She revealed a great sense of humor and started to dream about the future. By the time she was 87, she was saying, "I'd love to go to Norway, to visit my relatives there. But I'm so old. I've waited so long. I don't know if I'll ever get there."

So I took another risk. I told her if she wanted to go to Norway I would take her. She accepted my invitation instantly, and we went to Norway shortly after her 88th birthday.

While we were in Norway, we visited her cousins and camped in the mountains. Grandma was so happy, so enthused, that she was able to walk without the use of her cane and the wheelchair we brought. She didn't even want to take naps or go to bed at night because she didn't want to miss anything.

Her enthusiasm, her positive nature never diminished after that. In fact, she kept saying she wanted to go back to Norway when she was 95. My Dad and stepmother kept telling me, "You can't do it. She's 95. She's so old she may die over there." I loved Grandma's response. She simply said, with a twinkle in her eye, "Now that would be your problem."

ACADEMIC AND BUSINESS TESTS

At the same time I was having great success with the "brave question-20 question" technique, I was teaching it to my students. I taught them to ask their mother or father some brave questions when they were driving in the car together. Instead of their normal talk about dorm food, television, the college football team, and a paper they had to write, I asked them to ask some brave questions.

My university students came back with amazing reports. Some people reported having the best conversations they had ever had with their parents. Rather than talk on the surface about sports and activities, they learned about their parents' feelings, beliefs, fears, and dreams. It was a breakthrough in their relationships.

Jean shared her experience after hearing me speak at her financial company. She wrote to tell me about the impact of my seminar. In particular, she said the story of my grandmother and the brave questions stuck with her, and "I told it to my husband a few weeks later, when he was faced with a trip to Oklahoma to make a final visit to his dying mother. She was hospitalized with terminal cancer."

She said, "Dennis had not been on great terms with her since he'd left home at age fifteen. His real dad had died when he was two, and his mother had remarried when he was about eight. It became the classic story where Dennis suffered physical and emotional abuse at the hands of the stepfather while his mother did not protect him."

She continued, "He didn't know what he would say to his mother on his last and final visit. So I encouraged him to try the brave question technique. He and his older sister were with his mom when he asked, 'When were you the happiest?' She told them it was after their father had died and the three of them lived in a little house in Bloomington. She shared her memories. And from Dennis' description, it sounded like a beautiful moment for all of them."

But best of all, Jean finished her letter by saying, "After he returned, he said it was a wonderful visit. He reconciled with his mother."

In a similar fashion, I encouraged the participants in my business seminars to ask brave questions. If they were traveling to a conference with a colleague, I suggested that they ask a few brave questions of one another. I pushed them to go beyond the normal topics of quarterly reports and who wore what at the office.

Business people reported back to me. They told me how they achieved more understanding in a few minutes than they had achieved in several months back on the job. Instead of seeing one another as difficult people they wanted to avoid, they began to see each other as team members who needed support and understanding.

Tom was one such example. Tom attended my seminar for a pharmaceutical company. Some time later, he sent me the following email: "You really never know what is going on in the lives of your customers or coworkers. Your brave question technique taught me that. As a manager of twenty-five employees, I decided to try it. I shared some misfortune I was having and asked my employees some brave questions about their situations."

Tom said he started by telling his staff: "I have a two-year old son with a terminal illness which has no known cure. The fatality rate is 50% per year after diagnosis. So he is not expected to make it out of his early childhood years. A few weeks ago my mother was diagnosed with breast cancer. And it has taken me six months to tell you all this."

He said: "I then asked a few brave questions, and I learned some unbelievable things. I learned one employee has a 42-year old husband that needs bypass heart surgery. They have a 5-year old son. One employee has a father she cares for at her home that can not eat or care for himself. She leaves work and cares for him at night. One employee's mother has congestive heart failure, and they are investigating her options. One employee has an overactive thyroid that required surgery. She came out successfully but was told she may lose her speech. One employee's sister has breast cancer and requires a mastectomy. Another employee's sister has a bad heart valve and requires surgery to correct it."

"As a manager the lessons I have learned over the last year from this have changed me forever. We all have lives away from work. I've learned that employee performance issues may go much deeper than what I see on the surface. I've got to take time to develop relationships with my employees so I can bring out their best as well as be there to help them when needed."

In letter after letter, emails, and phone calls, the feedback was the same. Brave questions work.

THE RESULTS

I'm sharing my discovery with you because I know brave questions will also work for you. Brave questions dramatically improved the relationship with my Grandma, and it has dramatically improved all of my relationships since then. If you apply the same technique to your relationships on and off the job, you'll also see dramatic improvements in communication.

This book will show you how to do it, step by step. So now it's your turn.

Chapter Two

10 Guidelines for 20 Questions

You are about to enter one of the most exciting and valuable adventures of a lifetime—the adventure of truly open, honest communication. You'll be asking questions you've never asked before. And you'll hear answers you never would have imagined. In fact, you'll often be amazed at how little you actually know about your discussion partner.

Some people get a little frightened at the prospect of "deep" communication. Don't be. I'll show you a process for honest, open communication that is also safe and enjoyable.

Other people get a little concerned because previous conversations may not have gone very well. You may have gotten too side-tracked with certain individuals to have a productive discussion, and you may have found other individuals less than willing to ask or respond to questions.

Don't worry. I'll give you questions that people typically want to answer or at least find interesting and intriguing. And I'll give you some guidelines to keep you focused.

Still other people feel a little lost. They'll say, "I don't know what to ask" or "I just can't think of anything to talk about." Relax. You'll get so many brave questions in this book that it will take you hours, perhaps weeks and months to get through all of them. You'll have plenty to talk about.

In this book, you'll find twenty sets of twenty brave questions. They are grouped into various topic areas, and some may be more appropriate to use with some people than others. You decide. And some of the question exercises you'll want to use with several people. They're that good and that valuable.

It doesn't matter where you start. You can pick any one of the twenty question exercises. I'd simply suggest that you and your discussion partner agree on which set of questions you're going to use. Don't force the other person to go through a set of questions that he or she is unwilling to explore. The results won't be very satisfying.

You might want to use the brave question exercises like a "date." One week you choose the questions. The next week your discussion partner chooses the set of questions.

I've seen others use a set of questions as part of a "team building" experience. Whether it's a team on the job or at home, a group of people decide to work through a set of questions. They want to know each other better, or they want to live and work in greater harmony.

There are no hard and fast rules when you're asking and answering brave questions. However, I do have ten guidelines that I highly recommend. I've learned over the years what works and doesn't work in communication.

So here are the principles and procedures I recommend.

1. **Agree on a time and place to meet.**

    If you don't carefully choose the setting for your brave question discussion, you may be doomed before you start. You can't have a serious discussion when you're being interrupted every few minutes or where you can barely hear each other. For that matter, you can't even have a decent light discussion in a poor setting.

    Besides that, no one wants to feel put upon. No one wants to feel forced into anything. So don't "foist" these brave question exercises onto anyone. Don't push someone to answer these questions simply because you feel like it.

    Instead, tell the other person of your desire to give these questions a try. Ask when he or she would be willing to do that. Agree on a time that works well for each of you. Agree on a location that will be fairly free of distractions. And you'll be off to a good start.

2. **Commit to honesty.**

    As you go through the brave questions, there are no right or wrong answers. There are only honest and dishonest answers.

    The two of you need to commit to honesty right up front. You let each other know that whatever you decide to share will be the truth. That's the only way you'll build trust and understanding. In fact, if you can't commit to honesty, don't even bother with these brave questions. At best, you'll be wasting your time, and at worst, you'll be destroying your relationship.

3. Agree on your rules of confidentiality.

Some of the brave questions will reveal simple, fun, light information. Other questions may open up areas of discussion that you've never explored before. You may or may not want to keep your discussion just between the two of you.

That's up to the two of you. Just make sure the two of you agree up front. Is it okay to pass along what you learn about each other, or is it to be held in confidence? Make a specific, out-in-the-open agreement about that. Don't assume anything.

4. Go in sequence.

Try to answer each of the questions in an exercise, and try to answer them in the sequence presented. Don't skip around. The questions are arranged in such a way that you gradually move into deeper, more challenging topics.

Of course, you may find some questions too difficult or even impossible to answer. If so, just skip them. You can always go back to those questions at a later time—perhaps when you have more information, comfort, or trust.

5. Take your time.

Instead of racing through the questions as quickly as you can, take some time to give more thoughtful, comprehensive answers. You'll find that the pace at which you go will influence the effectiveness of your experience.

Remember, the number of questions you answer isn't nearly as important as how well you answer the questions. Whether you've got five minutes or five hours to spend on brave questions, make your discussion as real, authentic, and productive as possible. And that will happen if you take your time.

6. **Take turns.**

One of the first things you were probably taught as a child was to take turns. It didn't work well if one kid always went first, and it didn't feel good if one kid always hung back. It worked so much better if everyone was equally engaged.

The same lesson applies to brave questions. Take turns going first. Both you and your discussion partner should answer every one of the twenty questions in each of the exercises. However, you need to switch back and forth as to who answers a particular question first.

The easiest way to do this is to decide who's "odd" and who's "even." Flip a coin. The "odd" person initiates all the odd-numbered questions, and the "even" person initiates all the even-numbered questions. Again, you both need to answer every question. It's just a matter of who answers each question first.

7. **Listen; really listen to your partner's answers.**

Asking brave questions is a crucial skill that is needed in every important relationship and every work team. However, if you only ask questions and never bother to listen to the answers, you've accomplished nothing whatsoever.

I would suggest a few simple guidelines that will dramatically improve your listening. If you're seated, face each other and maintain fairly good eye contact. Refrain from looking at your watch or the things around you.

Then stay focused on listening and only listening. Don't get up to answer the phone, put away some dirty dishes, or file a paper. And don't say something as stupid as, "Go ahead. I'm listening" while you're doing something else. No, you're not listening. At least you're not doing your very best job of listening, and that's what's required by brave questions.

Finally, you need to occasionally paraphrase what the other person is saying. Simply rephrase in your own words the key points your partner is trying to make. He/she will know you're trying to understand, and he/she will know instantly if you do understand.

8. Don't think ahead or look ahead.

One of the biggest killers of effective communication is the "jump ahead." In other words, as your partner is talking, it's so easy to jump ahead of what he or she is saying.

Are you ever guilty of that? I know I am. Instead of listening to what is being said, I anticipate what will be said next or think about how I'm going to respond. In either case, I've stopped listening. And that's disrespectful and ineffective.

As you go through a set of 20 questions, you'll also be tempted to look ahead, to see what questions are coming up next. Don't do it! As soon as you look ahead, you start formulating your answer in your head. And while you're thinking about your answer, you're missing what your partner is saying at that very moment.

Stay in the present. Stay focused on what you or your partner is saying. That's all. Don't think ahead or look ahead.

Of course, this process will probably slow you down a bit. You may even have a few seconds of silence in your conversation as you think about your response. That's okay. It's better to really listen to your partner than blurt out an immediate response that may or may not fit with the conversation.

9. **Honor the right to pass.**

For brave questions to work their magic, you must be willing to give brave answers. You must be willing to take the risk of being a bit more open than normal chit chat.

However, you may come across a brave question you don't want to answer. That's okay. A particular question might seem uncomfortable or inappropriate. Just "pass" when those questions come up. Just say you prefer not to answer. You don't have to explain why, and your discussion partner shouldn't push you to explain why.

You each have to be the judge. You shouldn't be pressured into sharing more than you want to share, and you shouldn't pressure someone else into doing so. Besides being somewhat disrespectful, it usually doesn't work.

So honor each other's right to pass on a particular question. As your communication skills improve, as your relationship strengthens, as your trust continues to build, you'll find less and less need to pass on the really brave questions.

One caution. Don't use your right to pass as a cop out. If you pass on all the questions that fall outside your comfort zone, you won't make much progress in your communication or your relationship. I would suggest that you use the "help-hurt" guideline. If you think your answer to a brave question would "help" your relationship with the other person, go ahead and answer it.

10. Stop the discussion if it becomes unproductive.

Your time is valuable, and so is your relationship with your discussion partner. So if you find the discussion becoming too uncomfortable, if you're unable to concentrate, if things aren't going well, call "Time Out." Or continue the discussion as the two of you walk and talk. I've found that walking can ease the most difficult discussion.

If you decide to temporarily stop your discussion, agree on a time when the two of you will get back together. And then talk about any pitfalls you need to avoid. Then go ahead. Resume your questions. Your chances for a great discussion the next time around will be so much better.

If you follow these guidelines, you'll be quite successful as you go through the exercises in this book. You'll have a lot of fun. You'll learn a great deal about your partner. And you'll become a better communicator.

Chapter Three

Getting Started

W hen I deliver speeches and seminars, when I teach communication skills, people often ask me, "Where do I start?" Of course, the most obvious answer is to start at the beginning.

It may be that you've never had a chance to learn the skills of highly effective communication. You've never been taught how to ask questions or how to listen. And you've probably never heard of "brave questions" or engaged in a "20 question" exercise.

If that's the case, this is a good place to start. The questions in this section are less difficult or less "brave" than those found in later sections of this book. You'll get the practice you need here so you can be more effective there.

In addition to serving as a practice and a warm-up, this section is also helpful in getting to know someone a great deal better. You may want to build your relationship with a friend, relative, or coworker you've "known" for a long time. You may want to use the questions with someone you're just getting to know—whether that is socially or professionally. Either way, you'll find this is a good place to start.

Facts

Just Give
Me the Facts

*   *   *   *   *

This is a great place to start if you're unfamiliar with brave questions and not used to deeper levels of communication. In fact, this first set of questions would be appropriate with just about anyone. You'll get more acquainted as you get more adept in the art of communication.

As the title indicates, this set of questions focuses on the basic "facts" about you and your discussion partner. But you'll also have a chance to practice the skills and attitudes that comprise high-quality interaction. You will practice such things as gradually deepening self-disclosure, active listening, caring, acceptance, and feedback. Give it a try and see how well you can do. You may astound yourself.

1. What is your full name? How did you get that name?

2. What job do you hold? What jobs have you had in the past?

3. What was your neighborhood like when you were a child? How has it changed over the years?

4. What are some things you like about the place you live now?

5. Where would you like to travel if you could go anywhere? Why?

6. Where is the most interesting place you've ever gone?

7. What is one of your hobbies? What do you like about it?

8. What is a musical instrument you play or wish you could play? Why?

9. What is one of your all-time favorite movies? Why?

10. What makes you laugh?

11. What's something you do to relax?

12. What is your favorite time of the day? Why?

13. What would a perfect day be like for you?

14. What things cause you the greatest daily annoyance? What things bug you the most in an average day?

To ensure the success of your discussion, you must listen and listen well. So you should occasionally paraphrase what your partner is saying. Just rephrase your partner's comments in your own words as you understand them. It shows you care, and it shows you whether or not you really are "communicating."

So every once in a while, you need to use a phrase like this, "What I hear you saying is…"

Do it right now. Paraphrase what your partner just said.

15. **What is something you hate to do? Why?**

16. **What is one area in life where you excel?**

17. **What has been your greatest success in life?**

18. What talent do you wish you had?

19. What are three things you like about yourself?

20. What did you like about our conversation?

Your Yum-Yum Favorites

*　*　*　*　*

These questions may look deceptively simple. And on one level they are. They're not very risky. They don't reveal overly private information.

However, these questions reveal very important information about another individual—their "favorite" things in all parts of life. Indeed, I would suggest that you have to know these things about another person if you're really going to "know" or "please" that other person.

The fact is, most people don't know these things. They don't even know these things about their best friends and closest family members let alone their team members at work. The old TV show, "The Newlyweds," proved that. Couples who supposedly knew each other quite well found out they didn't know very much at all.

These questions would be appropriate with anyone of any age. They're fun. So try them out on several people. And if you want to have some extra fun, try guessing your partner's answers before he or she gives them. You might be surprised.

1. **What is your favorite color? Why?**

2. **What is your favorite food? What is one of your favorite desserts?**

3. **What is one of your favorite eating places outside your home? What makes it so special?**

4. What is your favorite TV program?

5. Who is your favorite cartoon character? Or what is your favorite comic strip? Why?

6. What is your favorite kind of music? Your favorite song?

7. What is your favorite leisure activity?

8. What would a perfect week-end be like for you?

Listening check: "What I hear you saying is…"

9. What is your favorite time of the year? Why?

10. What was your best vacation or vacation experience?

11. What would an ideal vacation be like for you?

12. What is one of the best gifts you've ever received?

13. Of all your material posses-sions, which one means the most to you? Which one gives you the most pleasure?

14. What do you most enjoy doing with your friends?

15. Of all the parties you've attended, which one was extra special? What made it special?

16. Over the years, which of your pets has been your favorite? Why?

17. What age do you consider to be the "prime of life?"

18. What is one of your favorite jokes?

19. What is your favorite saying? Why?

20. What was your favorite part of our discussion?

Tell Me a Story

* * * * *

Almost everyone loves a "story," adults as well as children. In fact, when people get together, a lot of their talk revolves around stories or the things they've experienced. Stories seem to capture our intellectual interest and our emotional excitement.

Stories also seem to be especially good at bringing people closer together. As we share our stories, we often find things in one another's lives that we can relate to. We find ourselves thinking, "I can identify with that," or "Yes, I've gone through something just like that."

As such, this set of 20 questions will work well with anyone on or off the job. These questions would even work in a group or team setting. Give everyone a chance to answer the questions, and you'll have a ton of fun. You'll also be a lot closer afterwards.

1. What is one of the most un-usual meals you've ever eaten?

2. What is the strangest restau-rant experience you've ever had?

3. When was the last time you were really surprised?

4. What's one experience you've had in losing something? Finding something?

5. When was a time when you personally got lost somewhere? What did you do?

6. When was a time you won something? Or earned some kind of reward? What was it?

7. What's one experience you've had in helping someone?

8. What experience or interaction have you had with another culture that has affected you?

9. What is one New Year's Eve you'll never forget? What happened?

10. What wedding have you attended that stands out in your mind as the most unusual?

11. What's the most unusual thing that has happened in your neighborhood?

Even if you ask good questions and listen well, not all communication is effective. Sometimes people give superficial answers, and some people go off on longwinded or irrelevant tangents. That and a hundred other obstacles get in the way of effective communication.

The good news is communication skills can be developed, and communication can be improved. The first step in doing so comes in the giving and receiving of feedback.

Quite simply, you need to stop your conversation once in a while and talk about how well the conversation is going. Talk about what is working and what could make it better.

Do that right now. Briefly discuss how this communication exercise is going.

12. **What is the funniest thing you've ever done as measured by the reaction of people at the time?**

13. What is one memorable bus, train, or airplane trip you've taken?

14. When did you ever have an experience in life where you just couldn't stop laughing?

15. What was a frightening moment that you've had?

16. What is one of the worst weather conditions you've ever gone through?

17. What movie brought tears to your eyes? Why?

18. What historical event has influenced you the most in life? Why?

19. What happened on one of the happiest days of your life?

20. What are two things you've learned about me through this discussion?

A Penny for Your Thoughts

*   *   *   *   *

Someone has estimated that the average person has 50,000 thoughts going through his mind each and every day. That's a lot. Some of those thoughts are innovative and creative while other ones are comfortable and familiar.

Of course, a lot of your thoughts are never mentioned. They never get discussed. And that's too bad, because your thoughts give a pretty good picture of you, your philosophies, and what you think is important.

This is a great set of questions to be used with anyone at anytime. You'll learn a great deal about each other without getting too "heavy."

1. What color comes to mind when you think of happiness?

2. What do you think makes a house a home?

3. If you could share one idea about raising children, what would it be?

4. How would you define success?

   Listening check: "It sounds like you're saying…"

Brave Questions

5. What qualities do you think are needed for success these days?

6. What is courage? When is fear ever appropriate?

7. How would you define "love at first sight?" "True love?"

8. What in your mind constitutes real beauty?

9. What do you think is the most beautiful place on earth?

10. What do you think about the possibility of life on another planet? Or extraterrestrial visits here on Earth?

11. What are the three top problems everyone shares?

12. Why do you think people use illegal drugs? What do you think should be done about it?

13. What do poor people need the most? What do rich people need the most?

14. What do you think has been the most significant thing that has been invented in your lifetime?

15. What do you think the world needs the most? Why?

16. What does freedom mean to you?

Listening check: "In essence, what you're saying is…"

17. What does your country mean
    to you?

18. How do you feel about war?
    How much do you think about
    it? When is it right or wrong?

19. What is a "good sport?"

20. What do you think we did well
    in our conversation? What do
    you think we could do better
    next time?

Chapter Four

Dealing with Timelines

*L*ife comes in chapters. And each chapter tends to be a chapter of time. You experienced certain things as a child, and you learned certain things as a child that shaped you and your life forever. The same is true for every other chapter in your life, whether that be your teenage years, adult years, or the years you anticipate.

This section focuses on the time chapters in your life. It encourages you to dig in and really explore one chapter of your life at a time. Some of the questions will evoke pleasant memories while others may evoke more somber moments.

Wherever you start, you'll be guided into a concentrated discussion that will be fun and rewarding. In fact, this may be the closest you'll ever get to time travel as you go back in time or jump ahead to the future. And I know you'll learn a lot about your discussion partner that you never knew before. Just remember, your focus is on understanding, not changing, your partner.

When You Were Just a Little Kid

*   *   *   *   *

*M*ost child development experts say that the first few years of your life are your most important years. Those years seem to have the most impact of any. They shape the kind of person you become, the way you see the world, and what you think and feel.

Besides that, it's just plain interesting to learn about the first few years of someone's life. You may have not been around your discussion partner when he or she was growing up, so these questions can open up all kinds of fascinating information. And children of all ages love to ask their parents these questions.

1. Where were you born? What, if any, unusual events surrounded your birth?

2. What is your earliest memory?

3. What was your childhood nick-name? How did you get it? How did you feel about it? How long did it stick with you?

4. What kind of house or apart-ment did you have as a child? What was the neighborhood like?

5. What kind of a child were you?

6. What was your favorite toy as a child? Your favorite game?

7. What was your favorite TV program? Why?

8. What was one of your favorite childhood stories?

9. What adult family members had the biggest influence on you as a child? How did they influence you?

Listening check: "So if I understand you correctly, you're saying…"

10. Which non-family members made the biggest impact on you as a child? What did they do?

11. How many brothers and sisters did you have? How close were you to each of them?

12. What stands out in your mind as being an especially good time you had with your family?

Feedback time: Briefly discuss how your conversation is going so far. What's working well? What could be improved?

13. What was Christmas (or some other key holiday) like when you were a child?

14. How did you feel about school during your elementary years?

15. What is one special memory you have of being in school?

16. When did you get into trouble as a child?

17. What was the saddest moment in your childhood?

18. What was the happiest moment in your childhood?

19. What is one thing you missed as a child?

20. What's one characteristic that you had as a child that you still have today?

When You Were Testing Your Teenage Wings

* * * * *

Lots of people sigh when they think about teenagers or their own teenage years. But that was an extremely important chapter in your life. It was a chapter filled with idealism, crisis, peer pressure, relationship building, identity formation, and a host of other important issues. So it's no wonder that people go to high school reunions 30, 40, or even 50 years after they graduate.

As such, these questions will open up a world you never knew existed in the life of your discussion partner. Some of the questions will bring laughter, and others will bring amazement. But you're bound to have fun.

Feel free to use these questions with anyone, although people from your personal life will probably find them more useful than other people. You might even want to use some of these questions for small group discussion when you have a reunion of some sort. Enjoy!

1. What were the popular fads and leisure activities when you were a teenager?

2. What kind of music was popular? What kind of clothing was "in?"

3. What was your high school like? Your college?

4. What activities were you involved with during your high school years? Your college years?

5. What did you do for money? How did you get money when you needed it?

6. What did you do in your spare time?

7. Who were your closest friends? How did they influence your life?

    Listening check: "And so the key ways in which your friends influenced you were…"

8. How did you deal with peer pressure?

9. What were some of your first experiences with dating? What was it like? How did you feel?

10. What three or four words would you use to describe yourself as a teenager?

11. How and when did you disobey your parents? Or those in authority?

12. What sort of crazy things did you do?

13. What was the most embarrassing thing that happened to you during high school or college?

14. Where did you go when you were down or upset? What did you do?

   Feedback time: Briefly discuss how open the two of you are being.

15. What were your goals when you were a young adult?

16. What was your greatest success as a teenager?

17. If you could relive one moment from your teenage years, which one would it be? Why?

18. If you could redo one situation from your teenage years, which one would you redo? Why? What would you do now?

19. What was your greatest learning experience during your teen years?

20. In what ways are you different today from when you were a teenager?

What I See at This Point in Time

* * * * *

Some motivational research says we perform exactly as we see ourselves. If we see ourselves as capable, for example, we work harder or try more than those that see themselves less positively. So understanding someone's self-perception is critical to understanding someone, who he is and why he behaves the way he does.

Strangely enough, however, the way a person sees himself is often quite different than the way others see him. That can be a source of curiosity or conflict.

In these 20 questions, the focus is on the present. The questions focus on how you and your partner see yourselves at this point in time. They're great questions to use with people you know well or people you don't know at all. And they work with friends and family as well as coworkers and team members.

1. What did you want to be when you were a child? How has that thought changed now that you're grown up?

2. What characteristics did you have as a child that have remained?

3. What characteristics have you lost or changed on reaching adulthood?

4. What is the best aspect of your personality?

5. What do you regard as your least attractive feature?

6. What movie star do you most identify with? Why?

7. How do others see you? How is that like or unlike the way you see yourself?

8. If someone were to write a book about you, what do you think he/she would call it?

9. How important is money to you?

10. What one thing would you like to have right now? Why?

   Listening check: Briefly discuss how well the two of you are listening to each other in this discussion.

11. What was one of your New Year's resolutions for this year?

12. What are the most important commitments in your life right now?

755

122*Dr. Alan R. Zimmerman*

71

13. Where are you, politically speaking, at this point in time? Liberal? Conservative? Etc.?

14. What health problems do you have?

15. What is one rut that you have in your life right now?

16. How could you improve your present living conditions?

17. How do you live your life—with planning and preparation or spontaneity and whim?

18. How is your life different today than it was 10 years ago? 5 years ago? 1 year ago?

19. Where would you like to be right now?

20. If we were to talk again, where would you like to go with our next round of questions?

What I See in My Future

*   *   *   *   *

There's a very insightful line in Lewis Carroll's book, *Alice in Wonderland*. One of the characters says, "If you don't know where you're going, any old road will get you there." And in today's world, it is said, "If you don't know where you're going, you'll probably end up somewhere else." Both comments are right on target. Thinking about and planning your future is an extremely important thing to do.

Of course, some people don't give much thought to the future. These questions will encourage such thought. And other people don't plan their futures. These questions will guide you in that direction.

You'll notice the questions are getting a bit "braver" in this section. They'll dig in a bit deeper. But it'll add an extra dimension of interest to your discussion. Go ahead and use these questions with anyone on or off the job.

1. How do you think the world will change during your lifetime?

2. What do you think the world will be like 100 years from now?

3. What goal would you like to achieve by the end of the year?

4. What will be one of your New Year's resolutions for next year?

5. What are three or four major goals you want to achieve before you die?

6. What makes you think you will or will not accomplish those goals?

   Listening check: "So what you're saying is…"

7. What do you want to learn or get better at in the upcoming years?

8. What kinds of adventures do you want to pursue in the future?

9. What do you want to be doing in 5 years? 10 years? 20 years?

10. How do you think your definitions of "success" and "happiness" will change in the upcoming years?

11. What would you like to see changed or improved in your personal relationships in the future? What will you do about it?

12. **What do you need to say to your loved ones at some point in the future?**

Feedback time: "How open are you being in this discussion? How satisfied are you with the depth of your discussion?"

13. **What "unfinished business" do you want to finish in the future?**

14. **How do you feel about growing old?**

15. If you had just one year to live, and had no financial restrictions, how would you spend the year? How would you spend the year if you had to live within your present financial situation?

16. What would you like people to say about you at your funeral?

17. How long do you think you'll live? Why?

18. What do you think will happen to you after you die?

19. Overall, how do you feel about "the" future? How do you feel about "your" future?

20. What can you do to make your future as bright as possible?

Chapter Five

Exploring Your Human Race

Everyone knows you're the product of your environment. And your environment is composed of the genetics you inherited, the experiences you've had, and the people you've known.

Well there isn't much that can be done about your genetic makeup. Previous sections of this book have addressed some of the experiences you've had. So let's take a look at some of the people who've influenced your life.

In particular, you'll focus on the friends and family members who've come and gone in your life. You'll get a chance to reminisce, think, and feel. And you'll get to really understand where your discussion partner is "coming from."

Family Roots
and Routines

$\mathcal{M}$any of the joys in life and many of your best memories have to do with your family. When you share certain activities or connect in some special way, life is really good.

On the other hand, many of the problems in families come from a simple lack of information. When people don't know something about someone, they tend to fill in the vacuum with assumptions and guesses—many of which are incorrect.

These questions will wipe out some of those assumptions. The questions are lighter in nature, but they'll get you started on the journey of discussing your family. You can use them with people in your personal life. You can even use them with children if you simplify the language. Dig in!

1. What state or country did your mother's family come from? How did that influence your family?

2. What is something your mother did that you do now?

3. What state or country did your father's family come from? How did that influence your family?

4. What is something your father did that you do now?

5. What is something you and your mother did together? You and your father?

6. How did your family celebrate birthdays? What was the best birthday present you ever received from your family?

7. How did your family celebrate the "holidays" when you were living at home?

8. What were three of your family traditions that you like and want to keep?

Listening check: "What I hear you saying is…"

9. What were your favorite things to do as a child? As a teenager?

10. How did you spend your Sundays when you were living at home?

11. What activities, besides eating, went on at the kitchen table when you were growing up?

Feedback time: Have a brief discussion about how you feel and what you think about your conversation so far. Agree on one thing you could do to make the second half of this conversation even better.

Dr. Alan R. Zimmerman

12. What did you do with your brothers and sisters when you were a child? Teenager?

13. Who was the "athlete" in your family? What did you/he/she do to become the "athlete?" How did that affect you?

14. Who was the "brain" in your family? What did you/he/she do to become the "brain?" How did that affect you?

15. How much time did you spend with your grandparents when you were growing up? How close are (were) you to them?

16. What is the most enjoyable thing you've ever done with your grandparents or older relatives?

17. What tradition did you enjoy sharing with your grandparents or older relatives when you were a child?

18. How are you like one of your grandparents? How are you different?

19. What member of your family do you most closely identify with? Why?

20. Amongst all your family roots and routines, what makes you the proudest?

Parental Influences
and Incidents

*   *   *   *   *

No matter how close you were to your parents in the past or how close you are today, your parents have a huge continuing influence on your life. So if you're really going to understand yourself or someone else, you've got to know something about those parental influences.

Of course, family "stuff" is very personal and often quite emotional. These questions require a greater willingness to be open than some of the other questions. You'll have to take a few more risks, and you'll have to go a bit deeper if you're going to have some truly meaningful communication. Don't shy away from the challenge.

1. What word or phrase would you use to describe your family?

2. How have you and your family been affected by a war?

3. How has divorce touched your family and your life?

4. What was something your mother considered very important when you were a child? What was something your father considered very important when you were a child?

5. What was a favorite saying of one of your parents?

6. What values did your parents try to instill in you?

7. How did your parents shape your spiritual or religious beliefs when you were a child?

8. How do your parents' beliefs and values play a part in your life these days?

Listening check: "The key thing I'm hearing is…"

Dr. Alan R. Zimmerman

9. What, if any, communication gap did you have with your parents when you were growing up? What about now?

10. When you were living at home, what subjects brought the most serious quarrels between you and your parents? What subjects bring the most disagreements today?

11. When did you get punished as a child? When did your parents criticize you as a teenager?

12. What is one deliberate lie you told your parents about a serious matter?

13. When did you feel the most loved?

Feedback time: Specify two things you like about this exercise.

14. What is a special memory you have of doing something with your mother? Your father?

15. How would you describe your mother's personality? Your father's?

16. What is one of the ways your mother and you are alike? Your father and you?

17. What one word would best describe your relationship with your mother? Your father?

18. If you could, what would you change about your parents?

19. What unanswered question would you like to ask your parents?

20. What is the one, most positive, most significant difference your parents made in your life?

Relative Changes
and Challenges

*   *   *   *   *

Someone said "everything's relative." And so it is. We're all connected in some way or other.

But some of your strongest, most important connections come from your relatives. After all, you not only share a somewhat common gene pool, you also shared many experiences over the years.

Your relatives changed you and challenged you. They served as role models, advice givers, and memory makers. And who you are today is partly a product of their influence.

These 20 questions will take you down memory lane. You'll have fun, but you'll also be pushed to think about some things you've never thought about. So you're bound to learn a great deal as you discuss these questions with friends and family members.

1. What activity do (did) you enjoy doing with your grandparents or older relatives?

2. What is one funny experience you had with a grandparent or older relative?

3. What is one story that has been passed on about one of your grandparents?

4. What was your favorite family celebration when you were growing up? Which one is your favorite today? Why?

5. Who is your all-time favorite relative? Why?

6. Which two family members most influenced your career? How did they influence you?

7. What is a habit you picked up from a relative?

8. Who is someone you lost in your family that was meaningful to you? How did that loss affect you?

Feedback time: Briefly discuss the quality of your communication so far and what, if anything, could be improved.

9. What is something your grandparents taught you? How is your life different as a result?

10. What unanswered question would you like to ask your grandparents?

11. What one thing do you like most about each of your brothers and sisters? Like least?

12. What one word best describes your relationship with each of your brothers and sisters?

13. What did you especially like about growing up in your extended family? Dislike?

14. Of all your relatives, which two have had the most positive influence on you? The most negative? How?

15. What family event or circum-
    stance in your growing-up
    years has had the most impact
    on who you are right now?

16. What has been one of the most
    difficult moments in your life
    with any one of your relatives?

17. When you think about all your
    relatives (brothers, sisters,
    aunts, uncles, cousins, etc.),
    when you think about your
    "extended" family, what are two
    thoughts that come to mind?
    What are two feelings you
    have?

Listening check: "What I'm hearing you say is…and I'm guessing you feel…"

18. **What do you like the most about your family these days? Like the least?**

19. **What do you wish your extended family would do more of? Less of?**

20. **What do you look forward to doing with your extended family?**

Circle of Friends and Foes

*   *   *   *   *

⊘ ne of the most frequent topics of discussion is other people. After all, "other people" have a direct bearing on many of the joys and many of the problems in life. As the poet, John Donne, said long ago, "No man is an island."

In this set of "20 Questions," you're going to talk about the non-family people who impact your life. Some questions are going to make you think, and some might even make you a little uncomfortable. If you're like most people, however, these brave questions will produce some very interesting answers and some very good discussion.

These questions will work with just about anyone. Go ahead and use them with people you're getting to know or know very well. They'll work in either case.

1. Who is one of the most interesting individuals you have met? What is so interesting about that person?

2. Who was the most influential teacher in your life? Why?

3. Which famous person do you wish you could spend some time with? Why?

4. If you could only take three people with you on a trip around the world, who would you take? Why?

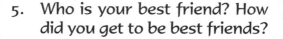

5. Who is your best friend? How did you get to be best friends?

6. How good of a friend are you?

7. What kinds of people do you most like to be with?

8. Who makes you laugh the loudest? Why?

9. When did you feel the closest to someone?

10. What is the first impression you make on other people?

    Listening check: "So you're saying…"

11. What do you think your friends say about you when you're not around?

12. How do you "use" your friends, in either good or bad ways?

13. When have you been "used" by the opposite sex? How did you feel? How did you deal with it? How does that affect you today?

14. Which people or kinds of people don't you like? Why don't you like them?

15. How do you feel about people who lie? How do you deal with people who lie to you?

16. How often, if ever, do you lie to other people?

17. What's one time when you really hurt someone's feelings? How do you feel about that incident today?

18. What is a communication problem you presently have with someone who means a lot to you?

19. With whom do you talk about your problems? Why?

20. What were the two best things about our discussion?

Notes

*   *   *   *   *

Jot down things you've learned and don't want to forget. Or write down some Brave Questions you want to ask in the future.

_____

_____

_____

_____

_____

_____

_____

_____

_____

_____

_____

_____

_____

_____

_____

Chapter Six

Digging in Deeper

Based on your experiences in the previous sets of "20 questions," you should be fairly good at asking and answering questions. And you should be fairly good at listening to one another, giving feedback on your discussions, and making changes in your communication if necessary. That's all very helpful as you dig into deeper, braver questions.

Of course, many of you are already quite skilled in communication. You didn't need the practice provided in the previous sections. You just wanted to learn the answers to some rather neat questions, or you wanted to build the relationship with your discussion partner. That's great. Either way you've received a lot of benefit.

Now it's time to stretch. It's time to ask braver questions that require braver answers. As Dr. Sidney Simon would say, such questions provide "juicier" discussions. They're the stuff on which deeper understandings are established and deeper bonds are forged.

Go ahead and stretch!

Mirror, Mirror on the Wall

*   *   *   *   *

Some people have difficulty talking about themselves. They'd rather talk about the weather, other people, or any number of topics that don't reveal too much of their inner workings. They're not comfortable talking about what's really going on inside themselves.

There are other people who talk about themselves way too much. They go on and on, sharing their thoughts on almost every conceivable topic. The problem is, much of their talk is superficial, and it may not be balanced with enough listening.

To get you beyond the superficial topics, to make sure you've got a balance between talking and listening, you're going to get 20 great questions in this exercise. You'll have to think. You'll have to be open. But you're going to get a lot out of this discussion as you talk to people at home, on a "date," or even as a part of a team building session.

1. If you had just one word to describe yourself, what would it be? Why?

2. How would you describe yourself to someone who doesn't know you?

3. What fictional hero do you most closely identify with? Why?

4. When you compare yourself to the way you were ten years ago, what comes to mind?

5. What full name would be more descriptive of you? Why?

6. What talents or special skills do you have?

7. How intelligent do you think you are?

8. On a scale of 1 to 10, how honest are you?

9. What moods or feelings best characterize you?

Listening check: "So the main things are…"

10. What do you regard as your best physical feature?

11. When do you feel the most proud of yourself?

12. What effect has fame, notoriety, popularity, or position had on you?

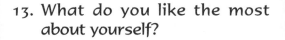

13. What do you like the most about yourself?

14. What do you most dislike about yourself?

15. What is something you sometimes pretend to be that you're not?

16. What was something you did that was "out of character" for you?

17. If you could be anyone, who would you rather be? Why?

18. When you are alone and no one can see you or hear you, what do you like to do?

19. How are you different on the inside than the outside?

20. What effect has this discussion had on you?

Turning Points
in Life

*   *   *   *   *

veryone can look back at certain events
and see how those events changed his
life forever. It might have been a chance en-
counter with a special person, or it might have
been a simple decision that had long-range consequences. Life gives the expected and the
unexpected.

And life gives you crossroad after crossroad.
Over and over again you have to choose which
direction you're going to go. And the choices
you make shape the person you become, the
life you live, and the future you will have. So
they're exciting, to say the least.

These questions look at some of the crossroads
you've encountered. You'll see how those points
in time became the turning points in life. Use
these thought-provoking questions with anyone you really want to know.

1. What was one of the proudest moments in your life?

2. What was your greatest athletic achievement?

3. What birthday was particularly special? Unforgettable? Why?

4. What was the most meaningful letter you've ever received? Why?

Listening check: "It sounds like you're feeling…"

5. What geographical move in life had the biggest impact on you? How did it impact you?

6. What was a time when it seemed like a new world opened up to you?

7. What is a major risk you've taken in life?

8. What is the hardest thing you have ever had to do in your life?

9. **What is something that few people know about you?**

Feedback time: List two things that are going well in your discussion. Decide on one thing the two of you could do to make your discussion even better.

10. **What is the stupidest thing you've ever done?**

11. **When were you the biggest disappointment to yourself or your family?**

12. What is a lie you often tell about yourself?

13. What is the biggest lie you ever told and ended up hurting someone?

14. What is one of the best decisions you made in life?

15. When feeling low or depressed, what do you do?

16. What is the best advice you've ever received?

17. When, if ever, have you considered suicide? Why?

18. What has been your experience with drugs and alcohol?

19. What was the most trying period in your life?

20. What event in your life has helped you/made you grow the most?

How the Spirit Moves You

*   *   *   *   *

Whether you call it spirituality, religion, values, or philosophy, most people have some very personal beliefs. Those beliefs may make up the very essence of a person, and they may be things that have never really been discussed. They're worthy of your time and exploration.

The trouble is, these are not easy things to discuss. Some people can get very pushy about their beliefs. They try to push other people into believing the same things they believe. Other people can get very defensive about their beliefs. They get all nervous when someone else disagrees with them. And still other people think their beliefs are so private that they never bring them out in the open.

These questions will help you avoid the pitfalls. They'll make it a bit "safer" to discuss such personal things, and they'll guarantee a fascinating discussion. Use them with some people from the personal side of your life. You won't be bored.

1. What is one memory you have of being in church/temple/synagogue as a child?

2. What is one good thing you were taught about God, church, or religion when you were growing up? One bad thing?

3. What has been the role of religious beliefs in your life?

4. What three things in life are most important to you now?

5. What value do you hold as very near and dear to you, a value that you would strongly defend?

6. What is your basic life philosophy?

    Listening check: "What I hear you saying is…"

7. If you could hang a motto or saying in every home in the world, what would it say? Why would you choose that one?

8. What in your mind are three of the most "immoral" things people can do?

9. When, if ever, do you think such things as swearing, cheating, and lying are ever justified?

10. What do you believe about God?

11. What do you believe about ghosts, spirits, and angels?

12. What mystical or supernatural experiences have you had?

13. What is one experience you've had that you would consider a miracle?

14. How do your spiritual beliefs contribute to your sense of peace? Security? Gratitude?

15. How do you feel when you hear about or think about death?

16. What do you think happens after you die?

17. If you were convinced reincarnation was a fact, how would you like to come back to life the next time around?

18. How do you feel about your spiritual life right now?

19. How do you want to grow or change spiritually?

20. What has been the most "spiritual" thing about our discussion?

Give Me Those Good Feelings

*   *   *   *   *

*W*hen you ask people what they want out of life, most people say, "I just want to be happy." Well that's great, but what do they mean? A thousand different people would probably name a thousand different things that bring about happiness.

Bottom line, people want to feel good. And there are a whole range of good, positive feelings in life. That's what this set of 20 questions is all about, about feeling good.

Of course, feelings are deeper than thoughts. They're more personal. They're more unique. They're a little harder to get a handle on, but once you do, you can expect a lot clearer communication and a lot stronger relationship. So these are great questions to use with people at home, on the job, with just about anyone anytime.

1. What's one activity that really makes you feel alive?

2. What things do you feel most grateful for?

3. What is guaranteed to make you laugh?

4. What gives you "goose bumps?"

Dr. Alan R. Zimmerman

5. What experience comes to mind where you were so excited you just couldn't wait for it to happen?

6. When did you feel especially proud of yourself?

7. When do you feel the most special?

Listening check: "It sounds like…"

8. What gives you the strongest feelings of security? How secure do you feel most of the time?

9. When do you feel the most content? Relaxed?

10. What gets you emotional?

11. What experience comes to mind where words just couldn't describe how you felt?

12. What three words describe how you feel right now?

13. When have you felt especially close to nature?

14. What is one situation where you felt extremely hopeful?

15. What has been the happiest moment in your life?

16. When was the last time you were so happy you cried?

17. What brings you the most hap-
    piness?

18. Who do you love the most?
    What do you love the most?
    Why?

19. When have you felt the most
    loved? The most loving?

20. In general, how did this discus-
    sion make you feel about
    yourself? About me? About
    anything else?

Oh No, I Hate Feeling This Way

*   *   *   *   *

Although it might be nice to have "good" feelings all the time, life is not that simple. In an average day, a person will experience many different emotions. And in a lifetime, a person will have to deal with thousands of "not-so-good" feelings.

According to some people, it is those difficult feelings that form—or at least reveal—a person's real character. In fact, if you knew everything there was to know about a person except their challenging feelings, you wouldn't really know that person at all.

As you go through these questions, you'll learn a great deal, but you'll also "feel" a number of things. You may feel amazed at some of the things you hear. You may feel sad when certain experiences are shared. And you may feel a lot of respect for your partner's openness and candor. These are excellent questions for getting closer to some of the special people in your life.

1. What feelings do you have the most trouble expressing? What is one time when you wanted to express one of those feelings but couldn't?

2. What emotions do you find the most difficult to control?

3. Which emotion frightens you the most?

4. What is your greatest fear?

5. What makes you feel frustrated? When do you get nervous?

6. When do you get jealous? Envious? What streaks of jealousy or envy do you have in your life right now?

7. What was one of your most embarrassing experiences?

8. How do you feel when someone laughs at you? What do you do?

9. When do you get lonely? How do you handle it?

10. What was your loneliest experience?

11. What turns you off the fastest?

12. What is guaranteed to anger you?

Listening check: "If I hear you correctly, the main thing you're saying is…"

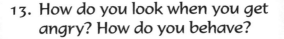

13. How do you look when you get angry? How do you behave?

14. How comfortable or uncomfortable are you feeling in this discussion? Why? What do you want to do about it?

15. What has ever caused you to feel ashamed?

16. What experience hurt you the most?

17. When was the last time you cried? How do you feel about crying in the presence of others?

18. What has been the most emotional experience you've had to deal with?

19. What feeling is most difficult for you to handle in other people?

20. What do you think I'm feeling right now? What do you think I appreciated most about our discussion?

Notes

*   *   *   *   *

Jot down things you've learned and don't want to forget. Or write down some Brave Questions you want to ask in the future.

_____

_____

_____

_____

_____

_____

_____

_____

_____

_____

_____

_____

_____

_____

_____

Chapter Seven

Talking to Your Partner

Asking people brave questions is always a bit risky. You're inviting them to reveal more of themselves than they might normally do.

However, it is an awful lot riskier to ask brave questions that focus on the relationship you have with your discussion partner. So many of those thoughts and feelings are kept inside, where they can do no good whatsoever. And some of those thoughts and feelings come out at the wrong time in the wrong way. Neither approach does much good in "building" a relationship.

This entire section is focused on questions you could and should be asking the closest person in your life—your spouse, significant other, best friend, or whatever you call that person. The questions are quite "brave" in nature, but they're very important. Without such questions, you get a relationship of the bland leading the bland, and you don't want that.

Of course, these questions might be outside your comfort zone. They should be. Just remember, these questions are made for understanding. Refrain from judgmental statements or attempts to solve problems. Refrain from interrupting one another. Your main task is to answer the questions openly and honestly as you listen with acceptance.

Understanding Our Walk Together

*   *   *   *   *

*T*he average couple spends less than thirty minutes a week in true, meaningful dialogue. What a shame!

Of course, they talk more than thirty minutes a week, but very little of that talk is about the deeper things in life. Very little of that talk is focused on feelings, needs, hopes and dreams, or the relationship itself. Most of the communication is about the kids, the weather, other people, or their jobs and activities.

People don't take the time to connect on a more intimate level. Or they don't know how to build their relationships.

Either way, this is a wonderful place to start. These questions will help you learn more about your relationship in the next few minutes than you may have learned in the last several years. And the more you learn about each other, the better chance you have of building an even better relationship.

1. What were some of your first impressions of me when we first met?

2. In what ways were those impressions correct? Incorrect?

3. When did you decide that you wanted a long-term relationship (friendship) with me? What made you decide that?

4. What three moments/periods have been the best in our relationship so far?

5. What are you most thankful for in our relationship?

    Listening check: "What I hear you saying is…"

6. What three moments/periods have been the most difficult in our relationship so far? What made them so trying?

7. What have you learned from our relationship that you wish you could tell newlyweds?

8. When do you feel the most loved in our relationship? The most special?

9. What "gifts" do you need from me?

10. How important is it to you that we continue to "date" each other? What kinds of things would you like us to do on those "dates?"

11. On a scale of 1 to 10, with 10 being the highest, how good of a partner do you think you are? What makes you think that?

Feedback time: Briefly discuss how you are feeling about this discussion so far. Specify one thing that would make you feel even better about the discussion.

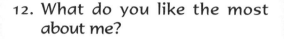

12. What do you like the most about me?

13. What do I do that "bugs" you?

14. What do you like the least about me?

15. What mistakes have you made in our relationship? Or what regrets do you have?

16. What do I say that embarrasses you or causes you to cringe or blush inside?

17. What do you think is most important for us to share?

18. What gets in the way of sharing your deepest feelings with me?

19. If you had just one minute to live, what would you like to say to me?

20. In what way do you feel differently about me or our relationship as a result of our discussion?

Building New and Better Roads

*　　*　　*　　*　　*

All progress is the result of change, but very few people like change. It's always uncomfortable, sometimes painful, and often difficult. That's why people don't talk about needed changes in their relationships, or if they do talk, the discussion is less than productive.

These 20 questions will help you out. These questions will get you into the "deep water." You will be asking some of the most important questions you could ever ask.

Go ahead. Grab a paper and pencil so you can jot down some of the critical answers you're going to hear. Get something to drink. And set aside a minimum of 45 minutes to meet in a quite place. It will be worth it.

1. When you look at our relationship, from the very beginning to this moment, how would you describe it?

2. On a scale of 1 to 10, with 10 being the highest, what number would you give our relationship today? Why? What could be done to increase that number?

3. What is your goal for our relationship? Where do you hope we will be in 5, 10, or 20 years?

Listening check: "If I'm hearing you correctly, you're saying…"

Dr. Alan R. Zimmerman

4. What do you think are my top three priorities in life? What do you wish would be my top three priorities?

5. What things would you like to see me throw out of my life?

6. What attitude would you like me to develop?

7. What achievement in my life would bring you the greatest joy? Would be best for our relationship?

8. What one thing would you change about yourself if you had a magic wand?

9. What do you need to change in the way you treat me? In the way you behave around me?

10. How important is forgiveness in our relationship? How well have we done in forgiving one another?

11. What's one area or issue over which you still need to fully forgive me?

12. What one thing makes you the angriest in our relationship? Makes you the angriest at me?

Feedback time: Talk about how satisfied you are with your answers to the above questions. Specify which of your answers, if any, you would like to change.

13. What's the most common mistake we make in our relationship? In our communication? And what can we do about it?

14. What could I do to make you feel more understood?

15. What can I do to make you feel more confident about our future together?

16. What mutual goal would you like to see us accomplish?

17. What are you most reluctant to discuss right now?

18. What, if anything, would you like to tell me that you haven't told me yet?

19. How well do you think we have communicated while answering these questions?

20. If you had a chance to do our relationship all over again, what would you change? What's our next step for making that happen in the future?

Wandering Along the Romantic Path

*   *   *   *   *

As the title implies, these questions are for people who are involved in an intimate relationship. They are to be discussed with your partner, not anyone else. And due to the personal, perhaps "touchy" nature of the questions, you might want to save this particular exercise until you've gotten fairly good at asking and answering brave questions.

Nonetheless, these are important questions. They need to be discussed at least once in your relationship, perhaps several times.

Just remember that these questions vary in terms of their intimacy. They start out a little easier, but they move to deeper, more personal questions. So It's especially important that you discuss the questions in the order they're given. Don't skip around. With that in mind, enjoy!

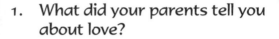

1. What did your parents tell you about love?

2. How did you discover the "facts of life?"

3. What events in your past have had the biggest impact on your thoughts and feelings about love? Romance? Sex?

4. How important is romance in a relationship? In our relationship?

5. What stands out as the most romantic or most special moment(s) in our relationship?

6. When do you feel the closest to me?

7. What could I do to make you feel more respected? More special?

    Listening check: "If I understand you correctly, the key things you need are…"

8. What would be your definition of an ideal, romantic time together?

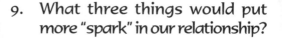
9. What three things would put more "spark" in our relationship?

10. When do you feel the most affectionate towards me?

11. On a scale of 1 to 10, how comfortable are you with touch? How do you like me to touch you? What don't you like?

12. How do you think our thoughts and feelings about sex are similar? Different?

13. If you were being really open and honest right now, what else would you say?

14. What seems to be the biggest block to our relationship getting better?

15. What do I do that turns you on? Turns you off?

16. When do you feel the most disconnected from me?

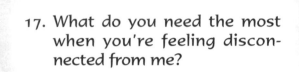

17. What do you need the most when you're feeling discon-nected from me?

18. On a scale of 1 to 10, how loving are you? How loving am I?

19. What could I do to make you feel more loved?

20. How did you feel answering these questions? Where do we go from here?

Chapter Eight

5 Ingredients of a Brave Question

By now you've probably gone through several of the "20 question" exercises in this book. But if you're like some people, you may have skipped those preliminaries. You wanted to create your own brave questions, or you wanted to dig in a great deal deeper.

That's okay, just as long as you do it in a way that works for you. After all, not all questions are effective. There's a big difference between good and bad questions, and there's a big difference between good and brave questions.

In essence, a bad question shuts down communication. A good question opens up communication. A bad question makes a person overly defensive. A good question makes a person more willing to answer. A bad question elicits a trivial or boring response. A good question elicits a comment of interest.

But brave questions go even further. Brave questions not only open communication, they open hearts. They raise issues as well as resolve them, and they elicit ideas and uncover needs.

So what goes into a brave question? Let me give you 5 ingredients. Include these 5 things, and you'll be quite successful as you make up your own brave questions and sprinkle them throughout your personal and professional conversations.

1. **Open-ended**

   Make sure your questions require more than a single-word response.

   Closed questions elicit one-word or one-phrase responses such as "Yes," "No," and "We'll see." They're good for getting the facts or getting to the point. And if that's all you want or need to know, they're okay.

   Closed questions are very common. You hear dozens of them every day. You hear such things as: "Do you like Italian food?...Do you agree with that program?... and...Are you okay?"

   Closed questions are not good for building relationships, however. They do not elicit the other person's opinions or feelings. And they do not deepen the understanding between you and the other person.

   By contrast, open-ended questions start with the five "W's" or one "H:" who, what, when where, why, or how. They require more than a single-word or single-phrase response, at least most of the time. They call for additional detail, explanation, or depth. And you almost always get more clarity.

2. Specific

General questions don't work very well. In fact, they often block communication rather than facilitate it. People don't know what to say when you ask too broad of a question, so they may not give much of an answer.

By contrast, brave questions are specific. They ask for specific thoughts, feelings, and experiences. That makes them easier to answer as well as more fun to answer.

Let's say you just returned from a trip. One of your friends asks you about it. He asks the general question, "How was your trip?" You'd probably think, "Ugh." It'd be too much work to fully answer that question. So you might say, "Fine," and leave it at that.

But let's say another friend asks you a specific question. She asks, "What was your favorite part of the trip?" Her question would give you some focus. You would know exactly what to say, and you'd probably answer it more comfortably.

So ask fairly specific questions.

3. Courageous

Good questions take a little thought, but brave questions also take a little courage. After all, you're asking questions you don't normally ask in everyday communication. So you can expect to feel a mite uncomfortable asking questions that are so much out of the ordinary. That's okay. Just recognize the fact that brave questions require more courage than "normal" questions.

It also takes more courage to answer brave questions. You will feel somewhat vulnerable sharing more of yourself than you usually do. You can't hide behind superficial answers or trite discussions about the weather.

And finally, it takes courage to hear the answers you're going to hear. You might not always like what you hear or agree with what you hear. But you will learn more truths in a short, healthy discussion than you might have learned in years of unfocused conversation. Those truths will become the basis for greater acceptance and team-work in the future.

4. **Honest**

    Brave questions bring out information. And a good dis-cussion of brave questions builds understanding and closeness.

    However, a lot of questions aren't questions at all. They're false questions. They make no attempt whatsoever to understand what the other person is thinking or feel-ing. They're disguised attempts to control or punish another person.

    If a boss asks an employee why she was late, but doesn't want to know the answer, she is being deceitful. Her ques-tion is simply an indirect way of expressing her anger.

When a father asks his son why he can't keep his room clean, he's not looking for information. He's not asking a brave question. He's indirectly ordering his kid to clean up his room.

When a wife asks her husband how the doctor would feel about his lack of exercise, when she knows full well the doctor has prescribed additional exercise, it's a deceitful question. It's manipulation. It's not a brave question looking for information. It's a disguised way of saying, "Get on the treadmill."

Make sure your brave questions are honest. Make sure you really want to know the answer. Any other hidden motivation is unacceptable.

5. **Constructive**

As you ask and answer brave questions, you'll talk about a lot of challenging issues, thoughts, and feelings. Some of the things you share will concern tough times, bad choices, and negative consequences.

You may not agree with some of the things your partner says or some of the things your partner has done. However, a good discussion is about respect and acceptance, not agreement and approval.

That means your questions must be motivated by a desire to learn more about the other person and build a better relationship with him or her. Your questions cannot be motivated by a desire to tear down the other person. That's destructive.

Let me give two examples. Let's say you ask someone, "When will you stop being so disrespectful of my feelings?" I don't think you want a full discussion of the possibilities. You're simply hiding behind a question as you tear the other person down.

Or you ask someone, "What's wrong with you anyway?" That's not a brave question either. It's not constructive. It doesn't try to build anything. It's simply an act of destruction.

As you create your own brave questions, take a moment to think. Ask yourself if your questions are constructive. Are you trying to gain some understanding? Are you trying to improve your communication? Are you trying to build a relationship? If that's your motivation, you're probably asking some very good brave questions.

Chapter Nine

Rules for Asking and Answering Your Own Brave Questions

You just read about the ingredients of a good, effective brave question. That's important. After all, you may enjoy your own questions more than the ones I give you. At least, you know which questions you really want and need to ask.

You may want to use brave questions as you take a walk with your spouse. You may want to ask brave questions as you ride in the car with your kid. Or you may want to ask brave questions as you lunch with a colleague. It doesn't matter.

What matters is that you do it "right." So it works for you. So let me suggest a few "rules" to follow.

1. **Agree on a time.**

    You may have some very good questions to ask, but your timing may be bad. If so, don't expect great communication.

Don't catch the other person off guard. If he is in the middle of a project, he'll probably feel irritated by your questions instead of encouraged. And if she's surrounded by other people, she'll probably feel like your questions are totally inappropriate. You want to make sure the other person is ready and willing to answer your brave questions.

And how do you know that? How do you know what is the best time to ask such questions? You ask. Ask if this is a good time. Or better yet, set up a mutually agreed upon time to go through some questions. It always works better to ask when your partner is ready to respond.

2.   Play fair.

You have the right to ask anyone just about anything you want to know. And others have the right to ask whatever they want. That's fair.

However, it's not fair for you to ask someone a question you're unwilling to answer. You've got to be willing to answer whatever you ask.

3.   Pave the way.

Even though you have the right to ask a question, your partner might want you to answer it first. That's okay. Your partner may respond to your question by saying, "I'm willing to answer that, but I'd like to hear your answer first."

By going first, you're paving the way for your partner. You're putting a measure of safety into the discussion. And that never hurts.

4. Ask two questions at a time.

Instead of you asking a question and then your partner asking a question, ask a pair of questions. Ask your first question. Listen to the response. And then ask a follow-up question that may or may not be related to the answer you just received.

After you've asked your two questions, switch roles. Let your partner ask you two questions. The use of the second question puts extra clarity and depth into your communication.

5. Pass if you wish.

The right to ask whatever you want also comes with the right to pass. You get to decide what you want to share. So answer all the questions you possibly can, but remember, you can refuse to answer if you wish.

That's it. Just five little rules. That's all you need to make brave questions work for you.

Notes

*   *   *   *   *

Jot down things you've learned and don't want to forget. Or write down some Brave Questions you want to ask in the future.

_____

_____

_____

_____

_____

_____

_____

_____

_____

_____

_____

_____

_____

_____

_____

_____

Chapter Ten

The Challenge

All too often, people complain about a "lack of communication." I hear that from individuals, from couples, from teams, and organizations. And they're right. A lot of the communication is insufficient or ineffective.

Now you know about brave questions. It's a simple technique for dramatic improvements in communication. I know it works. And so do thousands of others who have tried it and are using this technique on and off the job.

In the first chapter, I said the content of this book changed my life, and it will change yours. I trust that it has.

As you continue on your communication journey, just don't fool yourself. Reading this book won't do you any good. No book ever did that. The good always comes in the doing.

Go out and ask some brave questions. Get involved with a "20 question" exercise. You won't be sorry. In fact, you'll wish you would have known about this technique years ago.

Then drop me a line. I want to hear about your experiences with this technique. I want to hear your story. I want to hear about the great brave questions you've discovered, and I'll pass them on to others.

The best is yet to come!

Dr. Alan R. Zimmerman

About the Author

*   *   *   *   *

At age 7, Alan was selling greeting cards door-to-door. At age 14 he owned a small international import business. At age 21 he was teaching at the University of Minnesota, and during the next 15 years he taught interpersonal communication at two different universities. At both institutions, he was selected as the "Outstanding Faculty Member."

In 1985, Dr. Zimmerman opened his own speaking, training, and consulting company. That position has allowed him to deliver more than 2000 programs to more than a million people across the world. And he continues to deliver keynote, half, and full-day programs on a variety of communication topics to a variety of business, government, education, and health care clients.

On the personal side, Dr. Zimmerman and his wife live and work out of Minnesota in the summer and Florida in the winter. They have adult children, several grandchildren, and together they are actively involved in church work, hiking, biking, and international travel.

For more information about
Dr. Zimmerman's presentations contact:

Zimmerman Communi-Care Network, Inc.
20550 Lake Ridge Drive
Prior Lake, MN 55372
Phone: 1-800-621-7881 • Fax: 1-952-492-5888
E- mail: Alan@DrZimmerman.com
Web: DrZimmerman.com

Dedication

*   *   *   *   *

To my mother who always listened.
To my father who is always ready for a deep discussion.
And to my stepmother who always supports me.